• Dr Wouter H

LIFE IS
WONDERFUL
MAKE IT HAPPEN!

> This is an easy to read book, very motivating and encouraging. It is very much based on Dr Havinga's personal experience which makes it all seem achievable and realistic. I am sure it will appeal to anyone wanting to re-evaluate their priorities at work or at home.

- Dr John Hart, Course Organiser in General Practice

> For me, self help books have often seemed like flat pack furniture, somehow unfathomable and frustratingly complex. This manual comes ready assembled, it needs no tricky manoeuvres to get into action, and there are no vital missing pieces.

- Richard Aylward, Linguist

> It's a good read - very clear and concise. It re-emphasised a few things for me, and kept me on track. I've been writing endless lists and it's such a great feeling to tick achievements off. After 10 years of making excuses for myself, and hating cars, I am now learning to drive, and enjoying it.

- Amanda-Jane Strover, Recruitment Consultant

Acknowledgements

It has been a delight to write this book 'Life is Wonderful - make it happen!'. My inspiration comes from all the people I meet in my daily life, in my profession as a doctor as well as from friends and family.

I would like to thank:

My wife Nineke, who has always encouraged me to develop my own potential and who always has an unwavering belief in me;

my children, who are the real masters of life and will never fail to mirror the shortcomings in my reasoning!

my parents for their love, open-mindedness and their support of my decisions in life;

Richard Aylward, the language genius,
who helped me with the magic of language.

And thank you to all the authors and course presenters who gave me a template for my own ideas.

• Dr Wouter Havinga •

Contents

Acknowledgements	3
Introduction	6
Chapter 1: Wheel of Life	9
Chapter 2: Values	23
Chapter 3: Beliefs	29
Chapter 4: GROW	43
Chapter 5: Celebrate	51
Letter from Wouter	53
References	55

Introduction

As you read this book you will realise that you are on a journey and that it is you who is shaping that journey. You are in control and it is you who can turn it into a drag or featureless journey, but it is also you who can make your life wonderful!

Have you ever had your performance at work checked? What experience did you get from that appraisal? On the whole good, wasn't it? A proper appraisal should focus on what you have already achieved and that makes you feel good doesn't it? But that, of course, was only about reviewing your career. We all know that life is not only about a career, despite what others might like us to believe and probably above all, we tell ourselves. On top of this restriction we tend to focus on the negatives in life. However, there are many other areas in life than work and career, so in order to make life wonderful, I believe it is fundamental to reflect on other positive aspects too.

The ingredients

I am about to give you the ingredients you need to achieve a good, satisfying and wonderful life. It is up to you, however, to use them! The necessary ingredients to create a fulfilling life I have learned through my work as a family doctor, and in particular in my work at the Addiction Treatment Unit. It was there I trained in, and worked with, motivational interviewing techniques, solution-focussed brief therapy and building self esteem. Furthermore I trained in life coaching. This is about creating self-awareness in all areas of your life and setting goals to achieve the outcomes you want. Through life coaching you start to realise that your life is indeed a journey. And that it is you who can shape this journey into a wonderful one.

Throughout this book I will ask you to participate in various exercises. I will introduce you to the 'Wheel of Life', a tool which will help you to realise how fulfilled you are at this moment in time. Then we will start to look at what outcomes you want to pursue and follow this up with an examination of what makes us take certain decisions. This is important because decisions determine the direction we take in life. We will then go on to discuss the obstacles we meet on life's journey, as it is through these experiences we mature, in other words 'grow'. The letters G.R.O.W. are also an acronym for a system that helps in clear goal setting. At the end of this book I will show you and let you experience the 'Power of Thought'.

Chapter 1

The importance of setting goals

Let's start with how to take the direction of our life into our own hands, and I am talking here about setting goals.

☐ Are you in the habit of regularly setting yourself goals?

☐ Do you write your goals down?

☐ Do you know exactly what you want from life?

☐ Do you know your mission, your vision?

Every journey has a direction

Firstly, you need to know your destination. For example, when travelling you may go to London, or in my case Amsterdam, at times. You know where you are going.

At this moment in time you have chosen to read my book. You are doing this because you have set yourself this goal. It is the same with life; you should not step out of your front door and wander about aimlessly.

The following research, as the story goes, conducted at a business school in the sixties, illustrates how important it is to plan ahead and have written goals. Of all the students in their first year, only ten per cent had set themselves goals. Of that ten per cent, only half had written their goals down. Years later it turned out that the income of the five per cent who had consistently set themselves written goals was more than the incomes of the other ninety-five per cent taken together!

Not that earning lots of money is the purpose of your existence, but it does illustrate the powerful effect of setting yourself goals on a regular basis. It shows you the importance of having written goals.

But where and how do I start setting goals, you might ask? A way to plan your journey through life more consciously and consistently is by doing the Wheel of Life exercise regularly. In order to do so, I would like you to take a look at the 'Wheel of Life'.

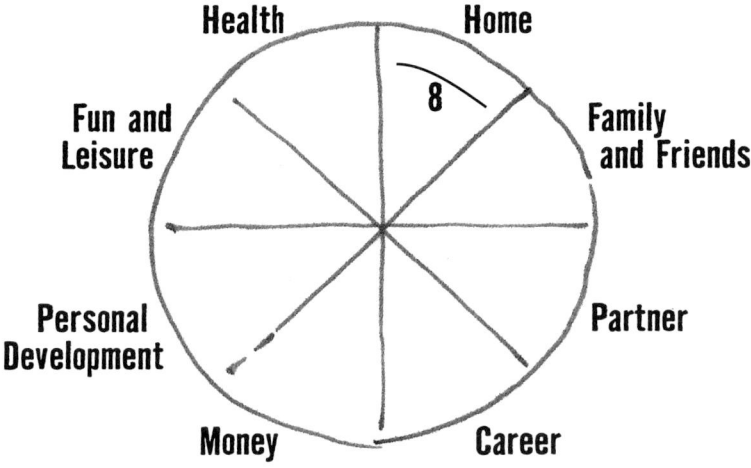

The diagram is also available from my web site
www.ISEEcoaching.com/wheel_of_life.htm

The circle is divided into eight areas, each indicating an aspect of your life. These areas are home, health, family and friends, partner, career, money, personal development, fun and leisure. Now, the big question is "What would a fulfilled life be like for me?"

On a scale from 0 - 10, with 0 being the centre of the circle and 10 the outer rim, indicate with a parallel line to the outer rim, how fulfilled you are in each of these areas. For example, if you rate your satisfaction in the area of your home an '8' than you can put that into the circle as indicated. Stop reading and do this now.

In all likelihood, a wobbly wheel will appear, because if you were to turn this wheel around it would give you a bumpy ride. And if you completed the exercise honestly then the image that appears will also give you an immediate idea of where you want to make positive changes in your life.

Life coaching is all about creating balance in your life. This might be a daunting prospect at first, but having arrived at this point in my presentations before an audience; I do a 'magic' trick with three pieces of rope. One long, one medium and one short rope and I show that it is very easy to turn these three unequal ropes into three ropes of the same length in a matter of seconds. This is to show that you too can immediately start to change things for the better for yourself. Look at the Wheel of Life you have filled it in - has it not given you awareness of where you can bring about a positive change?

The next step is to investigate which areas you want to make things better for yourself. I want you to highlight at least three areas where you want to make a positive change. Indicate these particular areas with an arrow pointing towards the outer circle. Start the journey - bring more balance to your life - make your life wonderful!

The next step is to choose one of your three areas and write down the outcome you want to achieve in that area. It is important to write down what you want, rather than what you do not want to put up with anymore. This is the trap that most people fall into. We are very good at complaining and talking about the things we don't like. In fact, this perpetuates the situation. Instead you need to focus on how you want things to be. For example, in the area of health, don't write, 'I want to stop smoking', or 'I want to lose weight'. These types of goals will not work in the long-term because once you have stopped smoking, for example, you will also have lost your goal and are likely to eventually start smoking again. Instead, write down what you do want to achieve. I have set myself the goal 'to have a fit, healthy and vibrant body'. There you go, that goal will carry me through the years!

Don't be reluctant to set yourself big goals. Failures are not possible in the game of goal-setting as you will always achieve outcomes.

You will always achieve a result and you can adjust each result further until you ultimately arrive at where you want to be. Often people get discouraged if they do not get the result they desire quickly, or when they get a negative answer from others.

Do you know the story of Thomas Edison and how he came to develop the light bulb? Well, the idea might have come in a flash but the product itself didn't come effortlessly. He developed his idea over a period of time and do you know how many attempts it took before he reached the final result? Well, his assistant yelled at him in frustration after the whole thing blew up on the 998th attempt and said, "Are you not fed up with all these failures?!" "No" Edison said, " I now know how to make an explosion, which may come in useful at some other time and each time I learn another way how not to make a light bulb." And, sure enough, after a few more attempts he was able to physically illuminate the world!
In other words, do not give up on you own endeavours, you are on your way to getting there.

Oh, but I am too old, I can hear some of you say. Well did you hear about Colonel Sanders? When he received his weekly pensioner's allowance, he looked at it and said to himself that it just wasn't enough for him. He had one asset and that happened to be a chicken recipe. He went off to restaurants and offered his recipe in exchange for a cut in the profit. And guess how often he was rejected before it started to take off for him? Give me a number - how many times was he told 'no' for an answer and yet despite these rejections kept pursuing his dream? Seriously, give me a number.

In fact it is similar number to the amount of attempts Thomas Edison made - over a thousand - and the result is the Kentucky Fried Chicken chain. So please don't say to yourself that you have proved to yourself something is not possible because you have had a few negative results, or that you are too young or too old. After these glowing examples, we should get back to the description of your goal in one of the eight areas that you have chosen. The goal should be worded in such a way that it describes how you want the situation to be and, of course, respect the freedom of choice of others and not involve you imposing your will on them.

So, how's it going so far? Is the Wheel of Life a helpful tool for you? Wouldn't it be a good idea to keep using this as a sort of barometer of your life and use it to help you set goals in the future?

The fourth step in the Wheel of Life exercise is to share what you are setting out to do. Talk to your spouse or friend and tell them what you have decided to do from today onwards. Start with sharing little plans. You will be surprised that they too have been thinking of undertaking things but were afraid to share them because sometimes people can be discouraging. These type of people tell you not to 'risk' certain things. These discouraging people may not like to see you do exciting things because they might start to lose you. They may feel that if you get a taste of freedom and get to know your true potential then you will be stepping out of your comfort zone and go off to do wonderful things. To them that means you will be moving away from their company - people do not discourage you out of spite but because they are afraid of losing you.

On the other hand, people love to see others who show courage to develop their true potential. That's why we all like to go and see a film and be emotionally touched by the actions of the performers on the screen. We love to get choked up, and you know why? Because we too are capable of the actions that are portrayed in front of our eyes. We recognise that potential is in us, only we hold ourselves back.

We tell ourselves that we are not good enough, or we are not worthy. Marianne Williamson captured that perfectly in her book 'A return to love'. Nelson Mandela even used her words in his inauguration speech:

> *"...our deepest fear is not that we are inadequate. Our deepest fear is that we are powerful beyond measure. It is our light, not our darkness, that most frightens us. We ask ourselves, who am I to be brilliant, gorgeous, talented, fabulous? Actually, who are you not to be? You are a child of God. Your playing small doesn't serve the world. There's nothing enlightened about shrinking so that other people won't feel insecure around you. We are all meant to shine, as children do. We were born to manifest the glory of God that is within us. It's not just in some of us; it's in everyone. And as we let our own light shine, we unconsciously give other people permission to do the same. As we are liberated from our own fear, our presence automatically liberates others..."*

How about it? Write down what little step, a practical step you can take towards reaching your goal. What can you immediately implement? Do that now. Write down what you can see yourself doing from now towards the realisation of your goal.

And when you have turned to your spouse, friend or neighbour and shared, you will also have experienced the power of speaking with another person. If you are passionate about your own life then keep it up and do not be discouraged if others do not respond in a way you had hoped for. Remember it was only your first attempt, a long way from a thousand! No doubt you will start to notice that after sharing your goal with another, you will find it easier to keep yourself accountable to what you have set yourself to do.

Even better is to set up a mastermind group! This is a group of like-minded people who meet up on a regular basis via phone, email or in person. Here you can share how you are getting on with your plans. A mastermind group will help you commit to your plans and give you support on your journey.

The saying goes, 'You have to do it by yourself, but you can not do it alone.' This is also what you use a life coach for. With a life coach you can propel yourself forward. You will purposefully work towards the fulfilment of your dreams. At the same time you will balance your life in such a way as to be less prone to stress and anxiety. Life coaching is carried out through weekly half-hour telephone sessions, so you do not need to go anywhere. It is done in the comfort of your own home.

Chapter two

Our direction in life

In order to understand what made you choose your direction in life, you need to know what drives you. What makes you do what you do? Write down what guides you on a typical day. Write down what factors influence you to do certain things. Yes, do that now, take a pen and write it down. For example, look at what rules your life at work or at home. What puts pressure on you? Do it now before continuing to read; write down the things that come to mind. You will benefit greatly by doing these exercises, so don't rush through these pages. It should not be an intellectual exercise but an experiential exercise. You will more easily get an insight to your life by allowing yourself to participate rather then standing on the sideline as a commentator. Participate and learn rather then lecture people or yourself. So find a pen and write down what things are controlling your life in a typical day, be it at work or at home.

Have you made your list with the things that sprang to mind? In that case read on.

What determines our direction in life? In fact, it is the values and the beliefs we hold about the situation we are in. These determine our decisions and our choices in life. Our decisions and choices determine our direction in life and these are based on our values and beliefs. So, it is not outside influences such as money, time, age or race.
This is a very important thing to know!

You will see that it is very important to know what we value in each of the eight areas shown in our Wheel of Life. What do you truly value? What is important for you in each of these areas? What do you care about? For example, in the area of your physical house, what do you find important there? For some of you it will be the quality and peace. For another, community or culture. Well, the first person is more likely to choose to live in the countryside whereas the latter would choose to live in a city with easy access to cinemas and theatre, for example. What about the area of career? What do you feel is important to you here? What do you need to experience in your career in order to be fulfilled in that area of your life?

People in a caring profession find it important to satisfy the sense of contribution. Many people feel the need to satisfy the quality of achievement, for others it is variety. You will notice that for each of us the values we hold are different. That is why we all do things differently. Your values and beliefs determine what you think, how you feel, what you do, what you say, the way you present yourself, your opinions, and just about everything in your life.

Examining the values you hold in all these areas is exactly what you would start doing when you begin with your life coach, because the values you hold are the blueprint of what you stand for.

Eliciting your values is actually a wonderful process because when you see these words, these qualities, in front of you, a most wonderful person will light up from that. It is heart warming to read these wonderful qualities because they describe the real you! And these will help to unveil your purpose in life.

The way to elicit your values is to ask for each area, 'What do I care about in this area?' 'What is important here?' 'What do I value here?' Try and keep it to one-word definitions; when you start to write a sentence to describe what you value and want to catch it in one word, ask the question, 'What does that mean to me?' 'What does that provide me with?' That is how you can scale it down to one-word descriptions. Write down at least three values for each area.

Some of the values you hold are more important to live by than other values - these values are called your 'core values'.

As I mentioned before, everyone holds different

values, and this can be the cause of friction. For example, if in a marriage one of the partners values security and the other adventure, then choosing a holiday together could pose a problem. The latter would perhaps like to go mountain walking whereas the other might prefer a hotel, a book and swimming pool. It is the same in your work environment when you are dealing with colleagues, superiors, staff or clients - be aware that others can hold different values to yourself. When you look at the situation from this point of view it is easier to come to an agreed solution.

First and foremost, being fulfilled or being stressed in your life depends on whether you stay true to your values or not. When you stay true to the values you hold then a fulfilled life will be yours. Fulfilment comes from being in alignment with your values but on the other hand, stress develops when you are not living up to your own values.

A simple way to make your life wonderful is to become aware of, and live by, your own values.

This is the first thing you will explore with a life coach. With your life coach you will clarify, investigate and examine the values that are important for you to align yourself with. I have explained this in more detail on my website, where you can sign up to my free life-coaching email course.
Visit www.ISEEcoaching.com/Ezine.htm
for more information.

Chapter Three
Every journey has obstacles

Now I will let you in on another secret: we actually make our own obstacles in the form of limiting beliefs. I asked you in chapter two to make a list of things that are obstructing you. You will see from your list that we often point to things outside ourselves but as I also mentioned, outside circumstances do not rule our life. In this chapter I will explain how limiting beliefs hold us back. It is what we believe about the situation we are in that rules our life. And I will explain how to change these limiting beliefs into enabling beliefs.

From childhood we are being conditioned. It is a fact that if you hear something at least three times then your brain takes it in as a solid truth and doesn't question it anymore. But these truths work like filters. You have installed these filters in order to protect yourself, and these filters make you respond according to that belief. The brain wants to maintain the integrity of your belief and it sort of goes out to look for evidence to confirm that belief. You can recognise beliefs because they sound like this 'I am like this...' or 'I can't do that', 'I have no time or money for this'. All of these beliefs influence the way you use your time and the responses you generate. They influence your opinions and your judgements, and the way you think, feel and act - indeed just about everything.

The saying goes, 'If you say you can, you are right and when you say you can't you are right too, but it is not about being right but about being happy!' In other words, you can choose what you believe so when you become aware of the fact that you are being held back by a limiting belief you can choose to change it into a belief that is more constructive for you. You can start to investigate how to convert it into an enabling belief. This is a belief that will support you in your quest. So, the obstacles are in fact our limiting beliefs and the good news is that we can chose to change these into enabling beliefs. The distinction between limiting beliefs and enabling beliefs and the effects they have on us are illustrated in the following story:

The story of two kittens

This is a story about two kittens who lived on a farm. One day they spotted a big bucket of fresh cream in their farmyard. Of course they couldn't resist the temptation and jumped straight in to kitty heaven! They gorged themselves on the cream so much that they then realised they couldn't get out because the edge of the bucket was too high. They became frantic to get out, splashing about to get to the rim.

The noise attracted the other kittens and they gathered around the top of the bucket. When they looked down they saw it was a lost cause and began to taunt the two kittens. They told them that they were foolish to jump in and there was

no way they would be able to get out, and would surely drown. But the two kittens kept trying until one of them took heed of what the other kittens were saying. He gave up the struggle and sank to the bottom.

The other kitten kept trying with intense determination and the belief he could get out if he tried, and - hey presto - the cream turned into butter and he was able to jump out. His friend was then able to wriggle his way out too, much to the other kittens' astonishment. They gathered around him and asked what made him go on despite their taunting. The kitten, surprised to hear what they were saying, replied by telling them that he was slightly deaf and that he thought that they were encouraging him to go on and not give up!

This story illustrates that it is actually you who can decide to take on a limiting or an empowering belief. Again, the saying goes, 'if you say you can, you are right and if you say you can't you are right too', but it is not about being right, it's about being happy!

Now let us examine your limiting beliefs. Go back to the obstacles you wrote down before (p.23). Investigate these statements and you will realise some of the limiting beliefs you hold. You will have some 'A-ha' experiences - that is actually why I called my website 'I See!'

One of the more common statements (beliefs) is that we feel limited by time, money, or work environment, but by holding these limiting beliefs you are telling your brain to shut off any other possibilities! You feel uncomfortable when things do not tie with your beliefs, so people look for the more comfortable situation. You expose yourself to situations that support your beliefs, in other words, you stay in your comfort zone. That is why limiting beliefs are obstacles to your growth in life. In fact, we always feel uncomfortable when we expose ourselves to situations that do not comply with how we view the world. However this uncomfortable feeling, this pain, means that there is also potential for growth. No pain, no gain! The pain notifies you of an opportunity where you can change the situation for the better, and rest assured, this pain is only short lived, whereas suffering is endured over a long period. Suffering means that you stick with an old belief and try to make the world adjust to you instead of you adapting to new circumstances and a new set of beliefs.

To recap on beliefs so far:

- a belief is a feeling of absolute certainty
- beliefs tell you when to feel pleasure and when pain
- there are enabling beliefs and limiting beliefs
- the choice is yours!
- when you believe you can, you are right. When you believe you can't, you are right too! But it is not about being right, it is about being happy.

When I give presentations to an audience I also perform a card trick and tell the audience that I am able to read someone's mind by observing the eye movements and posture. Then I ask for a volunteer to cut the pack and select a card so I can demonstrate that I can accurately tell what card was taken by the responses of that volunteer. This is always rather unnerving for that person because it feels very uncomfortable when you think that somebody else can read your mind. In such a situation you have the idea that the place of control is outside of you. Stress comes about when you have the idea that you are not in control so it is best to get that feeling of being back in control again. I then liberate the audience and the volunteer from this notion that I was mind reading by explaining that it was a magic trick after all.

It is liberating when you can let go of a belief that tells you that you are not in control - one that gives away power to another person or situation. It is important to develop the notion that you are in control, so if you have previously written that time is constraint, ask yourself how you can stop that belief. What is actually the issue here? Do you have difficulty saying no, difficulty delegating, do you need to change your job? How can you take control of the situation rather than try and control 'time'? Ask yourself the question, 'What would need to happen for me to...'

Choose your beliefs wisely. The choice is yours. Challenge and overcome your obstacles. This is what you would do with your life coach all the way through. A life coach is an independent person who questions you in a stimulating way. They help you to recognise limiting beliefs. As a start, I suggest you keep a diary of events and your responses.

About changing beliefs

Two things motivate us humans: we want to get away from painful things and want to move towards pleasurable things. The way to change a limiting belief is to attach pain to it. Ask yourself 'what is this belief costing me?' And, 'what have I lost having this belief?' For example, in your daily life, if you think that 'time' is limiting you, how is that affecting your communication with others or your concentration? Make a list and pile up all of those negative consequences! When you realise you lose out on a lot due to this limiting belief, you will gladly let go of it. When you find an empowering belief instead, ask yourself, 'what do I gain from having this belief?', 'how will my life change in a positive way when I live according to that empowering belief?'. Imagine and write down all of the wonderful things that can be yours when you start to live up to your empowering belief. Start to enjoy the pleasure and excitement that will follow as you are writing these down.

Unfortunately people tend to remain in their comfort zone. It is called 'being critical' and you will try and talk yourself out of possible improvements. Rather than face the fear of changing a habit and start doing things differently, many people take life as a routine and switch to auto-pilot. Many will even put up with domestic trouble or bullying at work. In other words often people are stuck in a rut and for them life is not so desperate that they have to change, but life is no real pleasure either. What a shame! You can make your life wonderful by taking on the belief that you can change it! Take control of what you believe.

Next, what belief would you like to have? Write down one positive and empowering belief you would like to have. And then write down how that enabling belief will change your life for the better. It's about becoming outcome focussed. How does it feel when you have arrived? What does that preferred state look like? How does it sound to you? For example, once you are in control of your time, how does that feel? What things will be possible for you? How does that change your life? How have things changed for you? What else do you notice? Or, once you have enough money. How does that change your life? What will tell you that you no longer have a lack of money? What will you see yourself doing that will tell you that you have money in abundance? What possibilities do you see appearing? How do you share this with other people? In general, how does your abundance, in every positive way, makes everyone better off?

By answering questions like these, you will arrive at the outcome you want. Describe the outcome in great detail and take yourself to where you want your life to be. Stop reading, complete this task and write it all down now!

You will have realised that sculpting your life is a very experiential thing. Take yourself to the situation when you have arrived. Ask questions that move you forward and make the effort to write it down and do that on a regular basis. Repetition is the mother of all knowledge and of every skill. So, if you want to develop the ability to do something well, like designing your preferred life, then keep practising at it.

Be bold

Have vision

Make life wonderful

Chapter four
GROW

I believe that the ultimate purpose of everyone's journey through life is to GROW.

We have now come to the penultimate exercise of this book and that is the GROW model. This model is a very powerful way of making things happen. It is used in most successful endeavours, for example by Olympic teams as part of their strategic planning, and particularly in joint ventures where common goals and action steps are essential for effective cooperation.

This GROW sequence can be a very effective tool in your personal life too. The G stands for Goal, R for Reality, O for Opportunities and W for Way forward. Let's start to use it and experience its power of effectiveness. It will help you to set clear goals and achieve the outcomes you want.

In chapter one I asked you to indicate three areas in your life where you want to make a positive change. Now take one of these and apply the GROW model.

1. **Goal**
2. **Reality**
3. **Opportunities**
4. **Way forward**

Goal

With reference to setting goals, most people will have heard about SMART goals. The S stands for Specific, M for Measurable, A for Action orientated, R for Realistic and T for Time bound. In other words, be specific in what you want. Describe it in detail.

You need to create a 'well formed' idea of the outcome. So, for example, setting the goal 'I want to be happy' is useless, because what does it mean specifically? To get a more specific idea, ask yourself what you see yourself doing that will tell you that you are happy. How can you measure it? 'Happiness' as a goal doesn't work because you can not put a number to it. However, you can create happy times for yourself! Dedicated time, for example, to have one or two hours during each week to doing something you have always wanted to do but have never got round to.

For me a SMART goal was to run a half-marathon. It's specific because I knew exactly what outcome I wanted - to run an official distance and be listed on an athletics website (measurable). It was action orientated because I had to train for it. It was realistic because I started jogging about two years before and had slowly built up my distance to run three miles a couple of times a week. It was time bound because I knew when I needed to do it by. In June 2003 I decided to train for the Stroud half-marathon which took place on the 26 October 2003, and here is my result! I am

number 1093.
http://www.stroudathleticclub.org.uk/half_marathon_results_2003.htm

All happy times make great stories of course, so let me tell you about my impressive finish. I made a massive end sprint to impress the crowds and my family at the finishing line. Like a spear I crossed the finishing line, only to notice afterwards that nobody had noticed me passing! Everyone was watching a runner who was vomiting on the finishing line. That made me think about how to draw attention next time but went off the idea to do the same after all. Instead I enrolled for the New York marathon.

Anyway, let's continue with the G in the GROW model. You now know that it is important to have a SMART goal. However, the biggest secret of goal settings is to set a positive goal. Most people set negative goals! I would like to reiterate what I wrote earlier because this concept is so important. For example, if you are overweight you probably think, 'I should lose some weight', but notice the negative word 'lose'. What is more, once you have lost the weight, you have also lost your goal! As a result you will soon start to put the weight back on. It is the same with, 'I want to stop smoking'. Notice the negative word 'stop'. Now you realise that once you have stopped, you have also lost the goal and might eventually take up the habit again.

Therefore, you have to set positive goals. The question to ask yourself is, 'How do I want the situation to be?'. Don't think how you do not want things to be. In the example of health issues, such as weight or smoking, you can set yourself the image of having a healthy, vibrant and fit body. This is a timeless goal. To put it differently, be careful with what you think about. Everything you put in your mind will be granted. The universe is abundant and gives you everything you put your mind to. Ask and you will be given. I once saw a television documentary of Jan de Hartog, a Dutch writer, and he said that his mother had warned him not to ask God for too many things, because what ever you ask for will be given! That scrambled my brain a bit as we usually think the opposite. Later I actually realised that we never ask, in fact, we always say what we don't want! For example, 'I don't want this stress', or, 'I don't want this kind of relationship. That made me think - and that is at the same time my caution - the universe is so positive that it can not hear any negative words like lose, stop, don't, won't, etc. So if you say 'I don't want this stress', the universe will give you 'stress', because it doesn't hear 'don't'. If you say 'I want to stop smoking', it will keep you smoking! If you say 'I want to lose weight', it will keep your weight!

Therefore, instead think about what you DO want. What positive goal will you set yourself for next week? Think SMART and think about what you DO want and write it down in great detail.

Reality

What is the situation like for you at present? Again describe it in detail. Who is involved? What is happening? What are you doing that you want to continue with in order to reach your goal? What do you realise you need to stop doing? What are you putting up with?

Opportunities

This calls for a brainstorming session. Without censoring yourself, write down as many opportunities that you see are available to you. Who can help you? Who can you ask? What outrageous possibilities can you imagine to support your cause? Just keep writing without telling yourself that some are ridiculous suggestions. This is best done walking! Be playful, allow yourself to think big! It is the opportunities that will help you to bridge the gap between your reality and your vision - your goal.

Way Forward

You can only get things done when you commit yourself to doing so. Therefore pin yourself down and actually set yourself a date by which you want to have something (what exactly?) done. Write it in your diary, pin it on the wall or stick it to your fridge, so that you see it everyday and are reminded of your commitment!

Once you have achieved what you have set out to do, you can add a N at the end of the acronym GROW. You have nailed it down and that is how you have GROWN.

If you have not celebrated your wins along that journey, then this is definitely a time to celebrate. Imagine you are going to do that, how you are going to pamper yourself? How are you going to pat yourself on the back when you have achieved what you have set out to do?

Chapter five
The Power of Thought

To finish I would like to ask you to participate in a very short exercise which takes only a minute but which shows, very dramatically, the power of thought.

Light a candle in a safe place and I would like you to sit up straight in a chair, uncross your legs and focus your mind on the flame of the candle. Next, close your eyes and concentrate on extinguishing the flame in your mind's eye after counting down from three and exactly on the word extinguish. Do this with your eyes closed, like this: 'three, two, one, extinguish'. Then open your eyes and see what has happened to the flame. It a very powerful exercise to experience the power of thought.

Okay, light a candle, sit up and close your eyes and focus your mind on extinguishing the flame.

'Three, two, one, extinguish.' Now open your eyes.

This exercise will definitely have shown that you have to take action to bring about changes in your life, rather than sitting around thinking, hoping something will happen!

In summary, in order to Make Life Wonderful:

1. Do the Wheel of Life exercise regularly
2. Set goals and write them down
3. Share what you set out to do
4. Be aware of what is driving you; your values and beliefs
5. GROW on your journey through life

and enjoy

A letter from Wouter

Time and time again I realise that life is to be enjoyed. You have an abundance within you, claim it and share it with others. Have fun. Live in faith, not in fear. You see, happiness equates with your capacity to love. Conversely, misery equates with your need for love. Instead of the latter, allow yourself to be this abundant and loving person and in order to be that way, love yourself and acknowledge your potential. Break out of your own confinement and shine. Know what you want and go for it! Let me know about your experiences, your resulting adventures, your fun and wonder of the magic that will happen to you once you are taking full responsibility for your life and are living it in a purposeful way. Send me an email!

Lots of love and best wishes

Dr Wouter Havinga

drhavinga@ISEEcoaching.com

Sign up for the FREE weekly life coaching email course, delivered to you weekly via www.iseecoaching.com/ezine.htm

This course will take you through similar material on a weekly basis. These weekly prompts will help you to move on and create the life you want.

Recommended reading

Feel The Fear and Do It Anyway
by Susan Jeffers

The Seven Spiritual Laws of Success
by Deepak Chopra

A return to love
by Marianne Williamson

Notes From A Friend
by Anthony Robbins

The Seven Habits of Highly Effective People
by Stephen R Covey

How To Get What You Want
and Want What You Have
by John Gray